My Simple Story

Hurt, Healing & Happiness

Written by Tiffany E. LaTerra

Copyright © 2015 Tiffany LaTerra
All rights reserved.
ISBN: 0692511997
ISBN-13: 978-0692511992 (Tiffany LaTerra)

My Simple Story

In loving dedication to mom. Sometimes I try on your wedding rings just to remember your hands carressing my face and whispering prayers over me as I pretended to sleep. Your beautiful spirit will forever live on in my dreams, memories, and family legacy.

To Dad, Josh & Dante. The strength of your masculinity encourages me to pursue a life worth living, facing every obstacle with visceral, enduring strength. Gwynette, you are the steadfast presence who has provided my family with unwavering love, and for that, I am eternally grateful. We are so blessed that your divine presence graces our lives.

Marj, your fervor and compassionate nature in life is the very medicine which heals my soul in moments where my mother is missed dearly, in moments where her love and guidance lives vicariously through you, providing my heart with inner solace. I'm so grateful she met you almost thirty years ago. Your role in my life has proven to be more than mom's best friend; You are my family.

And finally to my family and friends. Through life's most dramatic and profound obstacles and blessed moments of genuine bliss, your steadfast love and support makes me a better woman emotionally and spiritually. You know who you are.

Love you all.

My Simple Story

My Simple Story

Begin 10

Toil 15

Death 26

Love 32

Break 38

Fear 44

Relief 50

Search 58

Close 64

My Simple Story

Preface

"There are things in life we don't want to happen, but have to accept; Things we don't want to know, but have to learn, and people we can't live without, but have to let go." Unknown

I wrote this book with the notion, that perhaps my story will inspire hope to those of you who confront difficulties within your own lives. As I provide you a glimpse of my life with pure and profound sentiment, please understand that I am not providing a rendition of a guide to a perfectly happy life, nor do I carry a pretentious mindset to believe that my story is more devastating than that of any other human being. It is merely my desire to connect on a human level with the reader on the core basis of heartfelt emotions; grieving from loss and anger, as well as the re-discovery of happiness, freedom and hope, all of which remain re-attainable, even after such life altering circumstances.

"There are moments that mark your life. Moments when you realize nothing will ever be the same and time is divided into two parts, before this and after this"[i]

My Simple Story

Begin

It is an interesting place of conception when initiating a first book. Should I provide you the intricate details of my ideal childhood? Should I reveal the poignant intricacies of my pain? The contemptible nature of my sins? Should I provide you comical humor in the midst of heartache to evoke light-hearted appeal?

Perhaps I should employ the purest form of self expression and bare the naked aura of my soul unabashedly, without regard to the judgments of others, with the exception of the God who guides me from above. I must admittedly express that I have developed an innate fear over my writing capabilities, fearful of an inadequate outcome; contemplating my ability to convey my vulnerabilities to perfect strangers. Despite the inevitability of judgment or misconceptions, it is my passion within me that compels me to author this book through the passage of nostalgic thoughts and memory. The necessity of re-visiting my pain, in order to heal completely, provides a means of closure, reviving the fond memories close to my heart. The legacy of my beautiful mother will remain alive beyond the stillness of her ashes. It is imperative to remember that even beyond the devastating circumstances of life's obstacles, hope for a new day and purposeful meaning through joy and laughter add illumination to the darkest moments of our days. It is through the righteous passage of growing adulthood that I must discover the simplicity beyond my fears, and acceptance for my self-inflicted shame and guilt to honor the potential of greatness within me. I must follow my heart and share my life.

My life is nothing to be acclaimed. It is not spectacular by any stretch of the imagination. It does not encompass the emotional, physical, or mental anguish as the pain of those who fear for their lives from dawn to dusk. My life is incredibly blessed and I consider myself to be prosperous in intangible ways, in aspects unrelated to anything monetary.

For those who have sacrificed their lives to protect my freedom or those who have been martyrs to a worthy cause, that which affects my life appears seemingly insignificant. So why begin writing? Why decide to share? Because I believe at the instinctive core, each of us resonates on some level to the despair of fallen humanity; the empty heart that we feel in reverence to the loss of a loved one, that agonizing guilt we impose on our hearts with the pursuit of actions that may be considered shameful, the feeling of loneliness and vulnerability when all of our possessions have been removed from within our grasp. It is these human emotions that allow humanity to connect on a deeper level, where fellowship of the human heart is formed. It is through life's misfortunes that we discover a formidable strength within ourselves, a development of character through our moments of weakness, and an understanding of greater wisdom that will last us for ages. This is where my story begins, the tale of my loss, my grieving heart, my pain, and enduring strength.

At some level, I hope you connect with me and understand that dreams can come true and tribulations eventually subside with each passing day, as a testament of internal strength. I am sure many of you can relate in some aspect to the toil, loss, pain, laughter, fear, joy, and peace that I have experienced. If you discover aspects of yourself within this book, hopefully these pages and words will resonate with you, providing you the solace to know you are not alone. In the grand scheme of life, our seemingly greatest misfortunes may prove to be our greatest blessings in disguise.

The intention of my book is to reveal aspects of my tale while protecting my dignity, yet share enough of my story to encourage your soul, providing you a sense of hope that this too shall pass, enabling a sense of true empathy.

My Simple Story

My Simple Story

Toil

Growing up, we were very fortunate with our blessings, and as children, we were provided with all the things of which a person could ask. Of course, when you are young, you do not have the cognitive ability to fully comprehend the labor and sacrifices your parents must endure, to provide you with a life they find to be suitable for your well being. You are not made aware of their financial strife or the arguments behind closed doors, or even the capacity of the love they shared. It is true that ignorance may prove to be bliss.

We enjoyed long, summer afternoons catching frogs or building forts, swinging for hours, playing war or jumping rope, throwing a baseball around, while dreaming up winter adventures of skating and sledding, building jumps to fly into space. We were young, innocent and happy, and unaware of pain. We had everything we could ask for and more. As we grew older, the lap of luxury continued with daddy's gas card and shopping sprees at Nordstrom's. We would enjoy weekend trips to our boat in Mystic, CT, and enjoy mouthwatering New England delicacies on Saturday afternoons, while listening to the gentle lure of the waves, humming of peaceful serenity. Life was incredibly happy. Our strong Christian faith was the core of our beliefs, and we felt God had provided us with a plethora of blessings. As symbolism of our love and servitude towards his grace, our routines included fasting and praying, resisting luring temptations of evil. We were opinionated in our beliefs and determined to impose them on everyone we met.

2007 was the beginning of one of the most emotional and painful time periods in my young childhood. Life became hell on earth in our perfect little bubble of determined faith. I will never forget the image, forever engrained in my mind, of my mother showing me her breast. Her mammary duct had become infected. She was so worried and the anxiety was fixated in her eyes, but I attempted to reassure her, "Mom its fine. You're just going through menopause early. It happens to women." She remained spirited and we as a family remained strong. It was not until we began to see substantial loss in our business, that we became concerned. The new year of 2008 was quickly approaching, and things began to get stringent. Mom and dad began voicing concern of finances to my brothers and me. It became very apparent that the situational circumstances were declining, and with the demise of the housing market, the clients they once relied on for business were no longer able to acquire loans from the banks, which in turn, led to the decline of building projects. It was devastating to watch.

I vividly remember this specific night that I was eating dinner with my mother and father. By this point and time, we had already learned that my mom had breast cancer. I forget if dad or I had cooked, but we heard a knock on the door. There was a man standing there saying he had come to repossess our Audi. My dad in the calmest voice said, "Sir, my wife is sick with cancer and we are having great difficulty with our business due to the economy and we only have one payment left until we own it." He said he understood and would just tell the bank that we were not home. In this very moment, I remember feeling hopeless. Suddenly the responsibility of my family's finances became my own. I remember thinking, "I must do whatever it takes to help us survive." My dad shut the door and he held his head low, his facial expression was that of a man who felt desperation and defeat, a man who had worked so tirelessly, his entire life to provide for his family, only to watch his castle crumble before his eyes. He said to me "Stay with your mom, I'm checking the garage." The next thing I heard I would never forget; even now, as I recollect this moment, tears well in my eyes. My dad was infuriated, desperation and anger in his eyes. He ran into the kitchen crying and screaming, yelling and cursing. "They took the %$&^ car! They took the only thing I have left. I owed one more payment!"

I froze. I wept. I sat next to mom and it was in that pivotal moment that I realized I had to do whatever it meant to survive. I undertook the responsibility of the important bills. I began floating my bills, from one month to the next, submerging myself in as many hours at work as humanly possible, granting me the ability to contribute more money to our family. We began selling our things simply to stay afloat. Thankfully, my uncle was a saving grace and assisted my dad in retrieving our vehicle from repossession. Throughout this time period, we had many people who assisted us financially, paying for my mother's hospital bills from the cancer treatments. This began the cause of our financial demise in that time period, with the downfall of our business and an unexpected betrayal by a family friend of over 25 years. We lost our home in Connecticut and in North Carolina, as well as our boats and vehicles with the exception of the Audi, due to my uncle's generosity. It was then that I realized, that nothing in that time period could ever have mattered more, than the status of mother's health. I must make that blatantly clear. However, the loss of these materialistic, yet substantial things created excessive stress and pressure in the storm of this emotional and financial storm.

The stories I could divulge about this time period are seemingly infinite. I could express the compassion of how our family rallied around us, or how my co-workers in Charlotte wore pink ribbons (which to this day, still touches my heart at a capacity far more profound than words could ever describe), or I could reveal to you stories, about the checks we received in the mail from total strangers, willing to assist our family through these adversities. The stories I could tell you are seemingly endless. Yet, the recollection of such memories becomes painful to relive. Painful? How can giving and kindness be painful? I remember the tears my mom wept out of gratitude. I remember the sigh of personal relief I felt knowing I could provide groceries for my family. The recollection of such memories fills my heart with pain, because it brings my mother's living memories back to life. I remember her smile. I remember her anger. I remember her nightly prayers over me by my bedside. I remember her living. And on that spectrum, I also remember her passing. I will forever be grateful and indebted to those of you who assisted our family during this time; for helping, for encouraging us, for praying with us and staying by our side. I pray that many blessings may be bestowed upon your life.

My Simple Story

My Simple Story

Death

That week came, that miserable, awful, week. "Whatever happens I'm going to get my miracle." Those were the last words my mom echoed to my dad on the way to the hospital.

I received the dreaded call that we expected to head home to Connecticut immediately. So my brother and I headed home. My mom looked different. She appeared frail and sickly, as though she were a prisoner in a concentration camp. She was a prisoner to this disease, which they referred to as 'Triple Negative Breast Cancer'. Her radiance diminished when she began chemotherapy and radiation. Even now, as I write, I become enraged with anger and hatred toward chemotherapy and radiation. You must understand that my mom was healthy while doing alternative therapies, but once she was subjected to radiation, she passed away within a month. I understand every patient is different and I am not a physician, nor advocating one therapy above another, but for my personal story, chemotherapy and radiation left a detrimental perception within my life.

I remember my lively mother, lying incoherent on her bed, unable to communicate. The drugs the doctors prescribed "for pain" hindered her ability to speak to us.

The moment came when my father revealed he needed to speak with us. Even now, my stomach drops in deep anguish recollecting this scenario in my head. The three of us went into the waiting room and my dad collapsed on the ground. He told us the doctors stated it would come soon, and that if we placed my mother on life support, she would become a vegetable, enduring greater pain than she had already experienced. I'm sobbing now as I type; Sobbing as my dad and my brothers and I all sobbed that day in that ivory walled, cold waiting room. We held one another knowing we could no longer prolong her pain. It was her time to go home. It was her time to enter heaven before us and it was our time to mourn with deep, groaning pains over the woman who was our matriarch, our mother, dad's wife, a woman of great character, integrity and loyalty. She was the woman who bathed us and raised us to be strong, God fearing children, standing for what's right in the face of evil. She was my mother, my shopping buddy, and holiday menu planner, and so much more; her soul leaving this earth was imminent. She would not see me marry. She would not see my children. She would not know the pain I was to endure in the coming years.

My mom had departed us. It was about six o'clock in the morning when I felt my dad shaking me saying, "Sweetie, mom is gone. She went to heaven. She's dead." Even now, through my tears, I sob remembering this dreadful morning. Why did she leave this earth without us being by her side? Why did she go? WHY? God damn it WHY? I felt deaf and felt as though I could hear nothing. It was as though I was numb to the pain my body was experiencing. I remember my best friend being by my side, rubbing my back, with my dad holding me, as we were all sobbing. Even in this moment, I have to take a deep breath; the emptiness of her departure still overwhelms me and feels surreal. My breathing feels labored, even in this moment. My mother's soul had left us. I remember dad saying, "I was awake, I was awake until 3 am and she didn't wait for me to wake up to say goodbye. She chose to leave alone, without us by her side."

I must take a break to compose myself.

The days after mom passed away are seemingly blurry. I remember wanting to find her strength, so I could quickly recover, attempting to ignore my hurt and pain to find happiness once again. I remember my Grandpa and Grandma crying with us and I remember my Grandpa's hug. I remember shopping with my best friend, in honor of my mom, because I no longer had my shopping buddy. By this time, we had lost everything and could no longer afford shopping anymore, but the memories remain. What once was vivid, real life experiences had now become memories wrapped in a loving legacy. She was gone. She was ashes. She was now, forever to remain, only in my dreams.

My Simple Story

My Simple Story

Love

The virgin of thirty years had found love. I was head over heels in love. Mom had passed and I had transferred to New York City for my job; life appeared promising with opportunities before me. I was finding happiness in my new surroundings. I was ignoring God, ignoring my hurt, and ignoring my morals. After all, God had left me. He left my family. He betrayed us. We fasted and prayed righteously with our holy beliefs, attending church and youth group, as well as Christian school, and yet God had seemingly abandoned us. He ignored our hurt and diminished our suffering. He did not heal my mother, and therefore, I no longer cared.

I was blindly in love with a man who will remain nameless. He is nothing after all. I found him cheating on me, two years into the relationship. I am numb to this part of my life. I am numb in a good way; a healed way. When you don't understand dating or love, emotions tend to be escalated and dramatic when you catch the man of your dreams with another woman. I was devastated, to say the least. The only reason for revealing this aspect of my story is to reveal the role of this man in my life; he was the first guy I dated and the first guy who knew ALL of me. Shamefully, I admit this because I was raised to believe that I would find my one and only, and that would be it. At the age of thirty, with the loss of everything materialistic, the loss of my mom, and now the shaming loss of the man I thought I loved, I was a winner; a winner of shame and guilt, a winner of anxiety and grief, sorrow and loneliness and regret. I remember begging my brothers not to disclose the loss of my virginity, my purity, to my father. I stated that I was never going to be wanted; I felt nothing more than a common whore. That day was awful and grieving. I am not sure he will ever realize the capacity of pain and hurt he caused in my life, but after all these years, it may be seemingly insignificant. It was the chronological order of these events, my mother passing away and my boyfriend cheating on me, that made me incredibly angry with God. I remember throwing my middle finger to the sky, pissed that God had turned his back on us. I was angry and decided that caring about anything was futile.

A few months of chaos entered my life. I was exposed to things, of which I am ashamed, but do not regret. It was in this deep solitude of loneliness, that I found my true strength. I discovered the aspects of what I do and do not want in a relationship. My anxiety and panic attacks increased, only worsening my own health problems. My career began to develop. My confidence in my sex appeal began to increase. I began to develop strength that I never knew existed. I thought God had turn his back on me and never cared to know me again. It was when I experienced my first panic attack that I realized, "What are you doing? This has to stop. You can't live like this; always at the doctor, anxious, angry and hurt. You cannot become bitter. You can't."

From this point forward, I began seeking therapists and healthy alternatives. It was not until I discovered a counselor, who practiced EFT (Emotionally Freeing Technique), that I began seeing breakthrough in my life. I began healing. I began coping with my actions, understanding the pain I had accumulated deep within my heart. It was through this technique that helped me overcome many past, painful experiences, and allowed me to cope with my present pain more constructively. I began finding myself on the sunny side of recovery.

I do not care to disclose any more about the misfortunes in life. For I fear, it is pointless. Sometimes, we find strength in moving forward and moving on is exactly what I have done with my life. Living in the moment and moving forward is the best form of medicine and healing. When my soon to be ex-significant other cheated on me, my dad said, "He is nothing to us. Put on your heels and go back to Wall Street and kill it and find a trader!" I chuckle now to myself, but it was my father's way of being there for me, just as my mother would have been, had she still been alive. He gave me that comforting voice, reassuring me not to give up hope. I love my father very deeply.

My Simple Story

My Simple Story

Break

I had to take a few days off after writing the previous pages. Sometimes, even though this story is a compilation of events over the years, I find myself wrapped up in the exact moment of the tale, as if it were coming to life once again before my eyes. My emotions become pure, unadulterated, and in those moments, I must take the time to breathe.

Breathing can be incredibly soothing and necessary for the sanity of your mind or the sanity of your health. Breathing can allow troublesome stressors of the mind to be eased in such a way, where they are tolerable or diminished. Breathing can remind you of the good in life. The good, you ask? Is there any good left in this miserable life? I had my perception of what I believed to be good in life at that time. I had the good life with cars and boats and daddy's credit card. I had the good life dining in great restaurants, with moments of laughter, and Nordstrom trips with my mother. I had the good life getting massages at the Red Door Spa. Life was good when I fell in love and alive with my job.

My perception of all that was good in this world changed drastically when my mother passed away. The good that I saw in life diminished when we lost all of those frivolous possessions, things that I took for granted every day. Suddenly, the aspects of life that seemed so good to me all my life were now irrelevant. Now, I had more debt than I had in my salary. Creditors called my home asking for this person or that person. The only man I ever "knew" proved to be unfaithful with another girl. I felt trapped in a state I hated and a job from which I simply wished to escape. Life was no longer good; I had anxiety and panic attacks. I resented my life because life was no longer good to me. I knew the meaning of wealth; I once knew the value of nice things. I knew all these things never gave me true joy and I was never a materialistic person. It was just who I was at the time; it was simply the lifestyle I could afford, but now things have since changed.

After these years of tumultuous anger, sorrow, and emotional distress, I had no idea how to get my grip back on life. I knew something had to be done, because I could feel my health being adversely affected each day I awoke.

I was miserable.

Some of you may read this and think, 'well she had it made and then got a dose of reality'. And to some extent, I would agree with you. I was very fortunate, but in the nature of LIFE, someone else always has it worse or better; such aspects are easy enough said and very difficult to endure. In my personal experience, we were raised to live in this Christian culture, believing nothing bad could happen to a child of God. We felt blessed and had this idealistic belief that we were untouchable. We had victory in the name of Jesus and by his grace, we were healed.

It was this oblivious belief and doctrine, as well as my own misunderstanding that caused me to raise my middle finger to God and say, "How could YOU leave my family after everything we have done for YOU?" I felt betrayed by the most important, invisible man in my life. I felt as though my seemingly sinless life was now permeated with sin and disappointment and I no longer cared about a damn thing. I was angry at God, angry at life, angry my mother died without us around her, and angry that my life was encompassed by anger!

So what now? How do I get that feeling of happiness back again? How do I feel close to God even though I felt he was so far away? Is it even possible to recover from all of the loss? Was my broken, shattered heart ever truly going to mend? I felt like I had no way out. I felt overwhelmed with anxiety every day I awoke. I remember walking to the bus in NYC feeling as though I would pass out in the streets, and thinking, "well someone here will find me." I remember feeling so overwrought, with a deep sense of sorrow and grief; I honestly just wished to pass out, simply to be admitted to the hospital for a few days. But alas, I did not pass out. No one found me in an alley. I was just left to be miserable; wallowing in my pain.

My Simple Story

My Simple Story

Fear

I feel as though I must also talk about fear; fear of being open again, fear of being vulnerable, fear of loving, and fear that I shall never love again. My aunt said to me, "Isn't it funny how one person can have such power over you?" The thought of that sentiment made me pause for a moment. I thought to myself, "well he didn't alter me; the situation altered me." It compelled me to display an outgoing, funny, sarcastic, opinionated façade as a means of an emotional barrier, to allow no man to see that tender side of me again. I honestly, at times, fear falling in love again; when my mother passed away, I felt as though a part of my heart was ripped from my core. Two major events in my life, death and cheating, altered my perception of life substantially. These are painful situations for any person, but from my personal experience, it compelled me to put up an emotional wall to love. For those who have never experienced facets of love, it is a terrible and painful experience to endure, to love someone, only to have them ripped out of your life in such painful ways. I have finally found closure, in some ways, from the whole cheating experience. Truly, it was never meant to be and I thank

God that I discovered his infidelities sooner than later. What did scar me, however, proved to be the bliss my heart once felt, and the lack of consideration of a selfish person, whom I foolishly believed cared for me. I blame myself when I feel vulnerable again with other men, and when it doesn't work out or progress ideally, I continue to harshly blame my personal attributes. Often times in relationships, I feel as though my heart experiences anguish in the same manner, as when my mother passed away. I feel so alone, I feel afraid, and it takes everything within me to believe and reaffirm "This is not truth. You will love. You will be loved. It will happen and you just have to remember being vulnerable and feeling alone means you're healing."

Isn't it funny, how when we heal, we begin feeling scared and alone and vulnerable? Our past memories want to hinder us from moving forward. Our pain and anguish want to keep us from experiencing love, happiness, and freedom. It's as if a light bulb illuminates in my head, when I affirm positivity and love in my thought process. I feel peace. I feel the anxiety and emotional pressure in my mind diminish. The truth remains that we may all experience these simple steps in our lives. We all experience times where we feel insecure and alone, fearful and hurt, and angry beyond comprehension. These are not necessarily terrible feelings. These emotions that we associate with a negative connotation, may actually bring us healing if we allow ourselves to remain open minded. Understanding the value of feeling alone allows me to feel appreciation for the need of companionship. Fear drives me towards the pursuit of freedom. Vulnerability compels me to desire the experience of love. Whatever unfortunate experiences may come to pass in your life, please remember these negative feelings may inevitably provide you with a strength you never realized was an innate part of you, and a path of emotional healing if you are determined to commit to your spiritual journey of happiness.

My Simple Story

My Simple Story

My Simple Story

Relief

It was in these moments of anxiety that God began ministering to my broken pieces. I have always prayed, "Lord, no matter what, don't let my heart fall away from you. Never let me feel too far away."

I knew it was time for therapy. It was as though I had faced such an excessive amount of trauma, sorrow, and loss, I had to just stop and take life one day at a time. I finally made the decision to attend therapy, and upon arrival, I found myself just sitting there and sobbing. I laugh now at myself, because I felt such relief crying, yet so embarrassed by all my seemingly dirty secrets to reveal. After some time, I ultimately made the decision to stop attending. Perhaps, the idea that the first therapist was a man did not seem very appealing to me. He was a very nice man, who was very caring and genuine, but what my soul needed to heal was the motherly, nurturing type.

Even though I stopped attending my therapy sessions, my anxiety continued to rage with vengeance. My body was experiencing PMDD, IBS, and an array of unfortunate afflictions. I was always at the doctor. Growing up, my mother used to say that "everything is under the blood of Jesus and we were healed." We rarely ever had a necessity to see a doctor and when she became affected by cancer, I felt as though I was subjected to suddenly see a doctor every second of my life! Each physician diagnosed me with anxiety and/or hemorrhoids and an array of other associated symptoms. Apparently, the source of my afflictions required some much needed solace in my life.

I remember one nurse in the ER telling me I needed to calm down, after I had passed out. I felt like saying, "CALM DOWN?! CALM DOWN?! Do you have any idea what I have gone through?! Virgin for thirty years, who is a stereotypical good girl, who now lost her mom tragically to cancer, and then caught the love of her life with another girl, and now I feel like a shameless whore who will never be loved or healthy again! CALM DOWN my…" But no, I just sat on the hospital bed with my wonderful roommate telling me everything was going to be ok.

Okay. What is okay? Is it simply just learning how to cope with the pain, with which we have been subjected in our lives? Is it consuming anxiety pills daily and feeling like a zombie? Is it adjusting to hating where we are in life and just dealing with complacency? Is life just supposed to be this bottomless pit of anxiety, shame, horrors, guilt, and remorse? What the hell is OKAY?

It was all of these events that led to my search for happiness, true happiness, not induced happiness by means of pharmaceuticals such as Xanax (which for the record just made me feel so loopy I only took it, maybe twice, because I hated that cloudy loopy zombie feeling). Was happiness found in drinking or overindulgence in Ben & Jerry's? Happiness is ALWAYS found in Ben & Jerry's! However, for the purpose of my journey I wanted more than the expansion of my hips! I really wanted to find that balance of life; the balance where you say to yourself, "Okay. This is where you were. This is what happened. And this is where YOU are now."

So what did I do? I found another counselor! This time, I was acquainted with her from an internship I had attended in Texas. I had reached out to another woman I knew and she said I should go speak to this counselor. So this counselor and I began conversing. It was a comprehensive session of catching up real quick over the years, and then I blurted out, "Mom died, man cheated, I'm not a virgin, I'm pissed at God and I have health issues!" As we spoke, I felt relief and she began using the EFT technique on me.

What is EFT you ask? Well that's a great question! I'm not a doctor and can only tell you from my own personal experience. Emotionally Freeing Technique is where you essentially admit your feelings, while tapping certain meridian points on your body. It's simply balancing your emotions with your body's natural energy. For example, I would tap with my fingers on top of my head and say, "I caught douche bag boyfriend cheating." Then I would tap right above my eyes and on the sides of my eyes, saying something else that I was feeling, with my counselor guiding me the whole time. As I began this practice, I want to say my anxiety was almost 100% gone. With this practice alone, recovery was close to about 75% because it wasn't until I began supplementing with minerals, that I really noticed a substantiated difference with my anxiety relief. The recovery process is progressive, indeed.

For myself, tapping and talking to this female counselor and beginning to induce diet changes and exercise is what really helped me turn the corner. This went on for a few months and one Saturday morning I woke up and heard a whisper say, "Move to Florida." It was so audible that I called my best friend in Florida to tell her and she said, "Tiff start looking for jobs. You need some change and some good in your life."

My Simple Story

My Simple Story

My Simple Story

Search

The search for happiness began! I had already begun healing internally, from the pain of mom dying to the indiscretions of my ex-boyfriend, and now I had this gut feeling that it was time to do something for myself.

I would never want to bring any embarrassment to my family; however, when we were losing everything, I remember the weight of the financial burden being on my shoulders. I remember thinking that I had to provide and I had to pay the bills, and everything just felt so overwhelming. We were all coping with the aftermath of my mother's illness and losing our business so differently. I remember my dad and brothers having this huge, massive fight one night. If you ask me what it was about, I cannot even recall. The only word that comes to mind is stress. It was this excessive stress that became the catalyst reaction and friction within my family affairs, which made it even more difficult to endure.

All of my actions often caused secondary doubts, as I was always concerned about how it would it affect my dad and my brothers. It was at this point, I was beginning to feel the excitement of doing something for me! I began feeling as though I was becoming whole again, as if the world was mine to conquer! It seemed like I would just run into Mr. Right, my white Audi with brown leather interior would simply appear, and I would take myself and my family on a lavish vacation! The reality was that I began learning what it meant to embrace my pain, learn my "new normal," and let go of the past.

After six interviews, I finally nailed the job in Florida. I was so excited! I remember telling my aunt that I was so relieved and so excited to get to somewhere sunny! Living closer to the ocean just made me happy, even though my salary was substantially decreased.

So I made the move! My brother and I packed up the truck and headed south. I was so happy to be leaving my past behind and truly moving forward. I would also like to point out, that by this time, about 2-3 years had passed since my cheating experience, and about 3-4 years since my mother had passed. I was no longer running from my sorrow and pain. I was truly back on my feet and my healing process was at a point of allowing myself to be happy again. I am not sure we ever truly heal from our wounds when we are still on this earth, but I can say that I felt whole again. I felt whole enough to understand I was making a good move and evoking change in my life. I took control. I no longer allowed my anger, sorrow, and loss to control my daily activities. I was finally taking life by the balls! I was determined to change my circumstances so I could once again say, "I am happy!"

My Simple Story

My Simple Story

My Simple Story

Close

I'm not sure I can close this book. In life, there are no endings and I believe in our after life there are truly no endings. As I write this simple story, I find myself in sunny Florida with muggy days, Disney, beaches, and this day to day livelihood that I have created thinking, "what made me begin this book in the first place?" Perhaps, it was a funny feeling that someone, somewhere, would be encouraged by my simple story. Or perhaps, it's this inner voice telling me that we all have stories and most of us just never have the courage to reveal them. Usually, we sell ourselves short, believing our stories are meaningless.

But is that really true? Sometimes, we compare our own lives to those of others and think our pain is unlike theirs, stifling our pain because we think someone else may have it worse or that others just won't understand. But that simply isn't true! My simple story was not so simple to me. It was dramatic and complex, painful, embarrassing, and shameful. It was not the ideals of what a Christian woman "should be." Even writing this, I have left out certain disparaging details because I still have this

"I must be perfect stigma" in my head, which I feel obligated to achieve. I also have plenty of people in my life that have had no idea of my internal struggles. However, their encouragement and willingness to offer support and compassion was medicine to my soul, especially during these stressful times.

I can now say as time has passed, I have found a true relationship with God. I have realized that even though we go through difficult times, he truly does care for us and he puts people, places, and situations into play which affect our overall outcome for good. He is sovereign, and although we may not understand why we must endure such deep pain at times, God will take us through our journey to the other side. I can say I am in no way a perfect woman. I can say, I, by no means, have it all figured out. Some situations still remain difficult and others have blossomed into my favorite flowers. I have experienced the understanding and love everyone should experience from family and friends. I am blessed to be able to say, I am the most imperfect, happy, human being I can possibly be right now in life. I can also say I am not the same person I was fifteen years ago and I sure as hell hope I am not the same person fifteen years from now. My hope, in the word hope, has been restored and I look forward to the day I marry and have children, and vacation with no financial worries. I've also become a student of the Law of Attraction and other resources along those lines. It's encouraging to speak hope, happiness and life over my every day circumstances!

Our simple stories are simple tales with impacting differences. I've shared just a part of mine in hopes that my simple story will change your complicated life.

My Simple Story

My Simple Story

My Simple Story Wants Your Simple Story!

If this book has encouraged you or inspired you to want to share your own journey please visit http://www.mysimplestorybook.com to submit your story for future My Simple Story books! The goal is to have a variety of stories that bring hope and a sense of serenity to others who are going through similar circumstances. Categories include parenting, marriage, divorce, miscarriages, terminal illnesses, death, raising toddlers, raising teens, empty nesting, sexual abuse, career path changes, and possibly more depending on the submissions. The stories submitted will go through an editing process and must be appropriate for publishing and the author must email allowing for full disclosure. All other arrangements will be made as seen appropriate.

ABOUT THE AUTHOR

Tiffany Resides in Florida, enjoying the serenity of close proximity to the beach and other spiritually fulfilling activities. She finds peace in solemn activities such as writing, quilting, and cooking and enjoys spending time with those who have contributed positive guidance and love to her life. It is the profound moments of nostalgia, where precious memories of her late mother Julie, encompass the depths of her soul with happiness and laughter.

My Simple Story

References

Whitney, Gina. "Allison." LUCA : I Love the Way You Lie. Vol. 1. Gina Whitney, 2015. Print.

www.ingramcontent.com/pod-product-compliance
Lightning Source LLC
LaVergne TN
LVHW010017070426
835512LV00001B/2